BrainStrains

Sneaky
Lateral
Thinking
Puzzles

Paul Sloane & Des MacHale

Ⓢ

Sterling Publishing Co., Inc.
New York

Library of Congress Cataloging-in-Publication Data

Sloane, Paul, 1950–

Sneaky lateral thinking puzzles / Paul Sloane & Des MacHale
   p. cm.

ISBN 0-8069-8887-8

1. Lateral thinking puzzles. I. MacHale, Des. II. Title.

GV1507.L37 S5616 2002

793.73–dc21   2001049878

10 9 8 7 6 5 4 3 2 1

Published by Sterling Publishing Co., Inc.
387 Park Avenue South, New York, N.Y. 10016

This book is a compilation of excerpts from the following Sterling
titles: *Super Lateral Thinking Puzzles* © 2000 by Paul Sloane and Des
MacHale. *Ingenious Lateral Thinking Puzzles* © 1998 by Paul Sloane
and Des MacHale. *Intriguing Lateral Thinking Puzzles* © 1996 by Paul
Sloane and Des MacHale. *Tricky Lateral Thinking Puzzles* © 1999 by
Paul Sloane and Des MacHale. *Perplexing Lateral Thinking Puzzles* ©
1997 by Paul Sloane and Des MacHale.

© 2002 by Sterling Publishing Co., Inc.

Distributed in Canada by Sterling Publishing
^c/o Canadian Manda Group, One Atlantic Avenue, Suite 105,
Toronto, Ontario, Canada M6K 3E7

Distributed in Great Britain and Europe by Chris Lloyd at Orca Book
Services, Stanley House, Fleets Lane, Poole BH15 3AJ, England.

Distributed in Australia by Capricorn Link (Australia) Pty. Ltd.,
P.O. Box 704, Windsor, NSW 2756 Australia

Printed in China

Sterling ISBN 0-8069-8887-8

Lateral thinking puzzles present strange situations which require an explanation. They teach you to test your assumptions and help you to be open-minded and creative in your questioning. Clues for the puzzles begin on page 57. Answers begin on page 75.

A penniless sculptor made a beautiful metal statue, which he sold. Because of this he died soon afterward. Why?

A man was preparing a fish to eat for a meal when he made a mistake. He then knew that he would shortly die. How?

A foreign visitor to London wanted to ride up the escalator at the subway station, but did not do so. Why?

A golfer dreamed all his life of getting a hole in one. However, when he eventually did get a hole in one, he was very unhappy and, in fact, quit golf altogether. Why?

Why did a man write
the same two letters
over and over again on
a piece of paper?

What major scientific
blunder did Shakespeare
include in his play
Twelfth Night?

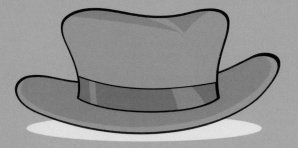

Why did the fashion for silk hats in the U.S. lead to an increase in the number of small lakes and bogs?

The ancient Greek playwright
Aeschylus was killed by a
tortoise. How?

A man stole a very expensive car owned by a very rich woman. Although he was a very good driver, within a few minutes he was involved in a serious accident. Why?

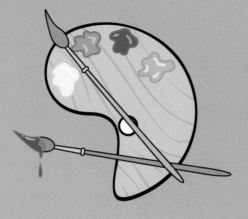

Leonardo da Vinci created some secret designs for his paintings that he did not want anyone to see. He hid them, but they were recently discovered. How?

Why did a woman send out
1,000 anonymous Valentine
cards to different men?

A man was driving down the road into town with his family on a clear day. He saw a tree and immediately stopped the car and then reversed at high speed. Why?

A mall café is pestered by teenagers who come in, buy a single cup of coffee, and stay for hours, and thus cut down on available space for other customers. How does the owner get rid of them, quite legally?

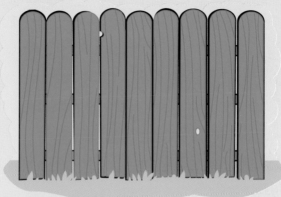

A man painted his garden fence green and then went on holiday. When he came back two weeks later, he was amazed to see that the fence was blue. Nobody had touched the fence. What had happened?

A man, a woman, and a child are watching a train come into a station. "Here it comes," says the man. "Here she comes," says the woman. "Here he comes," says the child. Who was correct?

Why did the vicar only want
a black dog?

A runner was awarded a prize for winning a marathon. But the judges disqualified him when they saw a picture of his wristwatch. Why?

Why are two little animals
alone in a little boat in the
middle of the ocean?

A famous dancer was found strangled. The police did not suspect murder. Why not?

A man standing in the middle of a solid concrete floor dropped a tomato six feet, but it did not break or bruise. How come?

A little shop in New York is called
The Seven Bells, yet it has eight bells
hanging outside. Why?

A man bought a pair of shoes that were in good condition and that fit him well. He liked the style and they looked good. However, after he had worn them for one day he took them back to the shop and asked for a refund. Why?

A man who was paralyzed in his arms, legs, and mouth, and unable to speak a word, wrote a best-selling book. How?

During fall, a little girl was in her backyard trying to stick the fallen leaves back onto the trees with glue. Why?

A woman heard a tune which she recognized. She took a gun and shot a stranger. Why?

A police officer was sitting on his motorcycle at a red traffic light when two teenagers in a sports car drove by him at 50 miles per hour. He did not chase them or try to apprehend them. Why not?

There is an orange in the middle of a circular table. Without touching or moving the orange or the table, how could you place a second orange under the first?

A young woman applied for a job as a secretary and typist. There were dozens of applicants. The woman could type only eleven words per minute, yet she got the job. Why?

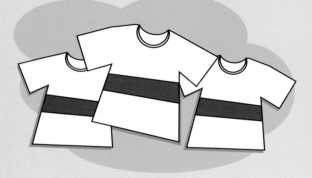

A change in the law in Italy resulted in large sales of white T-shirts with black bands on them. How come?

A man uses a stick to strike a part
of an elephant and after a few
seconds it disappears. The man is
then a lot richer. Why?

A man was building a house when it collapsed all around him. He wasn't injured or upset, and he calmly started to rebuild it. What was going on?

A meteorologist was replaced in his job because of a stuffed cloud. What's a stuffed cloud?

A keen ornithologist saw a rare bird that he had never seen before, except in illustrations. However, he was very upset. Then he was frightened. Why?

A horse walked all day. Two of its legs traveled 21 miles and two legs traveled 20 miles. How come?

Four people were playing cards.
One played a card and another player
immediately jumped up and started to
take her clothes off. Why?

A farmer has two pigs that are
identical twins from the same litter.
However, when he sells them he gets
100 times more for one than the
other. Why?

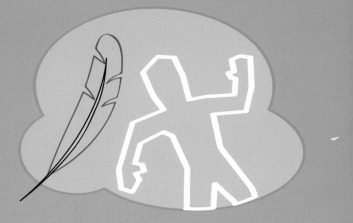

A man lies dead next to a
feather that caused his death.
What happened?

A man bought a beautiful and appropriate wedding gift for a friend's wedding. The gift was wrapped and sent. When the gift was opened at the wedding, the man was highly embarrassed. Why?

Adam was jealous of Brenda's use of a computer. He changed that by means of a hammer. After that, he could use the computer, but Brenda could not. What did he do?

There is a reason why men's clothes
have buttons on the right while
women's have buttons on the left.
What is it?

Two frogs fell into a large cylindrical tank of liquid and both fell to the bottom. The walls were sheer and slippery. One frog died but one survived. How?

A butterfly fell down and a man
was seriously injured. Why?

Why did a man who knew
the time and had two accurate
watches phone a clock that
speaks the time?

A man who did not like cats bought some fresh salmon and cream for a cat. Why?

A man undressed to go to bed and hundreds of people lost their jobs. Why?

A New York City hairdresser recently said that he would rather cut the hair of three Canadians than one New Yorker. Why?

A man is crowned king. Shortly afterwards, he is captured by enemy forces and chopped in two. Why?

Every time he performed in public, it was a complete flop. Yet he became famous for it, and won medals and prizes. People came from all over and paid to see him perform. Who was he?

Why has no one climbed the largest known extinct volcano?

Because it was raining, the firemen
hosed down the road. Why?

In a very exclusive restaurant several dozen diners are eating a top-class meal upstairs. Downstairs, precisely the same meal is being served at the same number of empty places where there is nobody to eat it. What is going on?

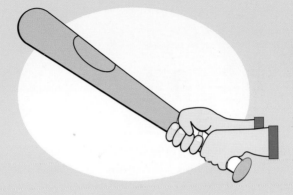

Why did a woman take
a baseball bat and break
her husband's fingers?

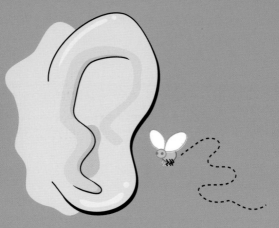

An insect flying into a girl's ear terrifies her. Her mother rushes the girl to the doctor, but he is unable to remove the insect. Suddenly, the mother has an idea. What is it?

CLUES

Page 4

He lived a lonely life in a remote building. He made the statue out of copper. It was taken far away and he never saw it again. He died as the result of an accident. No other person or animal or sculpture was involved.

Page 5

The man died in an accident. He was not poisoned or stabbed. No other person was involved. No crime was involved. The man did not eat the fish. The type of fish is irrelevant. It was dead. He was not indoors.

Page 6

There was no one else around. The foreign visitor saw a sign. He was very obedient.

Page 7

It was not a good shot that got him the hole in one. He should have been more careful. The golfer's ball rebounded into the hole. Another person was involved.

Page 8

He is not trying to form words or to communicate or send a message.
The man is working on a crossword puzzle.The letters he writes are S and E.

► Clues ◄

Page 9
The blunder did not involve physics, chemistry, mathematics, or astronomy. The blunder concerned the twins, Viola and Sebastian.

Page 10
The same environmental change would have occurred if felt hats or woolen hats had become very popular. More silk hats were sold and fewer other hats were sold. Fur hats were out of fashion.

Page 11
Aeschylus did not trip over the tortoise or slip on it. He did not eat it or attempt to eat it. He was not poisoned or bitten by the tortoise. No other human was involved in his death.

Page 12
Driving conditions were excellent, but the thief found the woman's car very difficult to drive. She had had the car modified. The rich woman suffered from some of the same frailties as other old people. There was nothing unusual about the car's engine, gears, wheels, steering, or bodywork.

Page 13
Leonardo hid the designs in a place where he thought nobody would ever find them, but they were not buried or locked away. People carefully stored the hidden designs for years without realizing they had them.

Page 14
She didn't know the men and didn't like any of them. She had malicious intentions. There was potential financial gain for her.

Page 15
There were many trees along the side of the road. The man had never seen or noticed this tree before. There was something different about this tree. His primary concern was safety. The tree itself was not a threat to him.

Page 16
The café owner did not change the menu or prices or music in the café. He changed the appearance of the café in a way that embarrassed the teenagers.

Page 17
No other person or animal was involved. The change in color was not caused by the sun or wind. The change in color was caused by the rain, but every other house and fence in the area remained unchanged in color.

Page 18
Do not take this puzzle too seriously—it involves a bad pun. The child was correct. But why?

Page 19
The fact that he is religious is not relevant. The vicar is particular about his appearance.

Page 20
The wristwatch was perfectly legal and did not give the runner an unfair advantage. The man had cheated. The clue to his cheating was that his wristwatch had changed hands.

Page 21
They were deliberately cast adrift from a famous boat. The animals can sometimes offend the senses.

Page 22
She was strangled to death with a scarf. No dancing was involved. She should not have been in such a hurry.

Page 23
The tomato fell six feet. It was a regular tomato. The man was fast.

Page 24
The shopkeeper could easily change the sign, but chooses not to do so. No superstition about numbers is involved. Many people notice the discrepancy.

Page 25
The shoes fit him comfortably, but there was something uncomfortable about them. They were made of different material from his other shoes. They were fine when worn outside, but not when worn inside.

Page 26
It was a long process. Somebody helped him. He used a part of his body that was not paralyzed.

Page 27
The girl is very sad. She is trying to prevent something from happening. She is acting on something she heard.

Page 28
She was in her home when this happened. She had heard the tune many times before. Normally she was happy when she heard this tune. The stranger was trying to rob her.

Page 29

The police officer was perfectly capable of chasing the teenagers and he was not engaged in any other task at the time. The officer was conscientious and always chased and apprehended those he saw breaking the law.

Page 30

The second orange goes under the first orange but the first orange remains on the table.

Page 31

She was chosen on merit.
She was a good typist.

► Clues ◄

Page 32

The T-shirts were designed to circumvent the law. The law was a traffic regulation. The black band was a diagonal stripe.

Page 33

The man is very skillful in his use of the stick. The man strikes something made of ivory.

Page 34

Although he constructed it with great care, the man thought that the house might fall down. He didn't intend that he or anyone else live in the house.

Page 35

The meteorologist died. He wasn't aware of the stuffed cloud. It hadn't affected any of his forecasts or reports. He was traveling.

Page 36

The bird was just as beautiful and rare as he had imagined. He wasn't disappointed with its appearance. What happened to the bird placed him at risk. He saw the bird through a small window.

Page 37

The horse was alive throughout and was not exceptional. The horse was a working horse. The two legs that traveled farthest were the front left and back left.

Page 38

They weren't playing strip poker and stripping wasn't a forfeit or penalty involved in the game. The actual card game isn't relevant. She took off her clothes to avoid harm.

Page 39

They were sold on the same day at the same market. Each was sold for a fair price. The two pigs looked the same, but when they were sold one was worth much more than the other. One was sold for food—the other was not.

Page 40

The man was physically fit and healthy. The feather had touched him. He was a circus performer.

Page 41
He was embarrassed with shame when his gift was opened. His gift wasn't offensive to the bride and groom in any religious, political, or moral way. He had bought an expensive gift but then made a mistake and tried to save money.

Page 42
Adam did not use the hammer on the computer. The computer was undamaged. Brenda had a disability.

Page 43
This is not a fashion issue. It has to do with right- and left-handedness. When buttons first came into use, it was the better-off who used them.

Page 44
The frogs were physically identical. One managed to survive the ordeal because of the result of its actions. The nature of the liquid is important.

Page 45
The butterfly was not a live butterfly. The man walked into trouble. The model butterfly served as a warning.

Page 46
He was not interested in the time. He wanted to make an innocuous telephone call. He was cheating.

Page 47
He wanted the cat to do something for him.

Page 48
The man was a movie star. The people who lost their jobs worked in the garment industry.

Page 49
The New York hairdresser had nothing against New Yorkers and has no particular love of Canadians. He charges everyone the same price for one haircut.

Page 50
Twelve men had started out in the attempt to become king. The one who succeeded was one of the few to survive.

Page 51
His performances were always a flop, but he was very successful. He was not in comedy, music, cinema, or theater. His most famous performance was in Mexico. He was a sportsman.

Page 52
It is not underwater—it is clearly visible aboveground. It would be very difficult to climb.

Page 53
They used regular water. The road was not contaminated in any way. It was for a special event. They did not hose the entire road.

▶ Clues ◀

Page 54
The restaurant is in an unusual location.

Page 55
She had good intentions.
He was in danger.

Page 56
The mother lures the insect out of her
daughter's ear.

ANSWERS

Page 4
He lived in a tower on a hill. Being poor, he had no money for materials, so he took the copper lightning rod from the building. He made a beautiful statue with the copper, but soon afterward the tower was struck by lightning and he was killed.

Page 5
The man's boat had capsized and he was adrift in an inflatable dinghy in a cold ocean. He caught a fish and, while cutting it up, his knife slipped and punctured the dinghy.

Page 6
The foreign visitor saw a sign saying, "Dogs must be carried." He did not have a dog!

Page 7
The golfer's ball rebounded off the head of another golfer who was crossing the green. The ball bounced into the hole. However, the man who was hit died.

Page 8
The man is given the world's most difficult crossword and offered a prize of $100 for every letter he gets right. He puts "S" for each initial letter and "E" in every other space. S is the commonest initial letter and E the commonest letter in the English language.

Page 9
The identical twins Viola and Sebastian are different sexes. This is impossible.

Page 10

Because silk hats came into fashion, the demand for beaver hats decreased. More beavers meant more small lakes and bogs.

Page 11

Aeschylus was killed when the tortoise was dropped on him from a height by an eagle who may have mistaken the bald head of Aeschylus for a rock on which to break the tortoise.

Page 12

The rich woman was very nearsighted, but did not like wearing glasses or contact lenses. So she had her windshield ground to her prescription. The thief could not see clearly through it.

► Answers ◄

Page 13
Leonardo hid the secret designs by painting over
them with beautiful oil paintings. He knew that
no one would remove such masterpieces. But he
did not know that modern X-ray techniques
would allow art historians to see through the oil
paintings and reveal his designs.

Page 14
She was a divorce lawyer drumming up business!

Page 15
The man saw a tree lying across the road. He
was in Africa and he knew that blocking the
road with a tree was a favorite trick of armed
bandits, who then waited for a car to stop at the
tree so that they could ambush and rob the
passengers. He guessed correctly that this was
the case here, so he reversed quickly to avoid
danger.

Page 16
The café owner installed pink lighting that highlighted all the teenagers' acne!

Page 17
The man had made green paint by mixing yellow paint and blue paint. The blue paint was oil-based, but the yellow paint was water-based. Heavy rain had dissolved the yellow paint, leaving the fence decidedly blue.

Page 18
The child was correct. It was a mail train!

Page 19
The vicar wears black suits and knows that light-colored dog hairs will show up on his suits, but that black ones will not be noticed.

Page 20
A picture of the runner early in the race showed him wearing his watch on his right wrist. When he crossed the finishing line, it was on his left wrist. The judges investigated further and found that one man had run the first half of the race and his identical twin brother had run the second half. They had switched at a toilet on the route.

Page 21
The two animals were skunks that had been ejected from Noah's Ark because of the stench they were causing.

Page 22
The famous dancer was Isadora Duncan, who was strangled when the long scarf she was wearing caught in the wheel of her sports car.

Page 23
He caught it just above the ground.

Page 24
It was originally a mistake, but the shopkeeper found that so many people came into his shop to point out the error that it increased his business.

Page 25
The man found that the synthetic shoes generated a buildup of static electricity when he wore them around his carpeted office. He constantly got electric shocks, so he rejected them and went back to his old leather shoes.

Page 26
He winked one eye and thereby indicated to a very dedicated assistant each letter, word, and sentence of the book. He was Jean-Dominique

Bauby, the French writer. The book he wrote by blinking, *The Diving Bell and the Butterfly*, was published just before his death in 1996 and became a best-seller.

Page 27
The girl has a fatal disease. She overheard the doctor tell her mother that by the time all the leaves have fallen from the trees she will be dead.

Page 28
The woman was alone and asleep in her house in the middle of the night when she was awakened by the sound of her musical jewel box. She knew that a burglar was in her bedroom. She reached under her pillow, pulled out a gun, and shot him.

Page 29
The teenagers were traveling on the road that crossed the road the police officer was on. They drove through a green light.

Page 30
Put it under the table.

Page 31
Typing eleven words per minute is going quite fast, if the language is Chinese!

Page 32
A law was introduced making the wearing of seat belts compulsory for car drivers and passengers. Many Italians tried to circumvent the law. They wore the T-shirts in order to give the false impression that they were wearing seat belts.

Page 33
The man is playing billiards (or snooker or pool) with balls made of ivory. By pocketing a ball with his cue, he wins the match.

Page 34
The man was building a house of cards.

Page 35
A stuffed cloud, in pilot slang, is a cloud with a mountain in it. The meteorologist was a passenger on a plane that hit a stuffed cloud. He was killed and had to be replaced at his job.

Page 36
The ornithologist was sitting on a plane coming in to land when he saw the rare bird, which was sucked into the jet engine causing the engine to fail and the plane to crash-land.

Page 37
The horse worked in a mill. It walked around in a circle all day to drive the millstone. In the course of the day, its outer legs walked a mile farther than its inner legs.

Page 38
When one player went to play a card, she knocked over a mug. The hot drink poured over the other player, who immediately jumped up and started to take her clothes off.

Page 39
This happened in France. One pig was sold for bacon. The other had been painstakingly trained to sniff out truffles and was, therefore, very valuable.

Page 40
The man was a circus sword swallower. In the middle of his act someone tickled him with the feather and he gagged.

Page 41
The man selected a beautiful crystal vase in a gift shop, but he knocked it over and broke it. He had to pay for it, so he instructed the shop to wrap it and send it anyway. He assumed that people would think that it had been broken in transit. Unfortunately for him, the shop assistant carefully wrapped every broken piece before sending the package.

Page 42
Brenda was blind and she depended on her Braille manual when using the computer. Alan flattened the pages with a hammer.

Page 43

Most people are right-handed and find it easier to fasten a button which is on the right through a hole which is on the left. This is why men's buttons are on the right. When buttons were first used it was the better-off who could afford clothes with buttons. Among this class the ladies were often dressed by maid-servants. The servant would face the lady, and so it was easier for right-handed servants to fasten buttons that were on the lady's left.

Page 44

The frogs fell into a large tank of cream. One swam around for a while but then gave up and drowned. The other kept swimming until his movements turned the cream into knobs of butter, on which he safely floated.

Page 45

The butterfly was made of plastic and was put on a large plate-glass window to indicate the presence of the glass. After it fell off, a man walked into the window and was seriously injured.

Page 46

The man is having an affair. Once he has phoned his mistress, he calls the clock so that if his wife should later press the redial button she will not find out anything he does not want her to know.

Page 47

The man was a television cable engineer who needed to thread a cable from the back of a house, under the floor, to the front. He released the cat with a string attached to it into a hole at the back of the house. The cat was lured by the smell of the cream and salmon to find its way under the floor to the front of the house. The string was used to pull the cable through.

Page 48
The man was Clark Gable, the screen idol, who took off his shirt in a movie in which he was about to go to bed. He was not wearing an undershirt. So great was his influence that men stopped wearing undershirts and factories making them had to close down. In a later movie, he wore an undershirt and restored it to fashion.

Page 49
He gets three times as much money!

Page 50
This is normal in a game of checkers (or draughts).

Page 51
His name was Dick Fosbury, inventor of the famous Fosbury flop, a new high-jumping technique that involved going over the bar backward and that revolutionized the sport. He won the gold medal in the Mexico City Olympics in 1968.

Page 52
The largest-known extinct volcano is Mons Olympus on Mars.

Page 53
This incident occurred just before the start of the Monaco Grand Prix race, which is held in the streets of Monte Carlo. Part of the course runs through a tunnel. When it rains outside, the firemen hose down the road in the tunnel in order to make the surface wet. This improves consistency and safety.

Page 54
It is the first-class restaurant on a luxury ocean liner. Upstairs is out on deck. If it rains the entire company transfers downstairs and takes up where it left off.

Page 55
He was holding a live electric cable. The electricity had paralyzed the muscles in his arm. Her action freed him.

Page 56
She put the girl in a darkened room and placed a bright light near her ear. The insect emerged.

If you liked this book, you'll love these other Paul Sloane and Des MacHale books from Sterling:

Challenging Lateral Thinking Puzzles

Great Lateral Thinking Puzzles

Improve Your Lateral Thinking Puzzles

Ingenious Lateral Thinking Puzzles

Intriguing Lateral Thinking Puzzles

Perplexing Lateral Thinking Puzzles

Super Lateral Thinking Puzzles

Tricky Lateral Thinking Puzzles